God and Me

This Little Light of Mine, I'm Gonna Let It Shine!

Asia Coleman

God and Me
Copyright © 2023 by Asia Coleman

All rights reserved. No part of this publication may be reproduced, distributed, or transmitted in any form or by any means, including photocopying, recording, or other electronic or mechanical methods, without the prior written permission of the author, except in the case of brief quotations embodied in critical reviews and certain other non-commercial uses permitted by copyright law.

Tellwell Talent
www.tellwell.ca

ISBN
978-0-2288-9228-1 (Paperback)

YOU ARE FEARFULLY AND WONDERFULLY MADE

Psalm 139:14

In the beginning God
created me and I'd knew I
would be someone great.
                    Jeremiah 29:11

For I know the plans
I have for you.

When I dream, I dream of all the adventures I will go on. Like flying into outer space and seeing all the things God has made.

Psalm 8:3

When I look at your heavens, the work of your hands, the moon and the stars, which you have set in place, I know there is a God.

One day when I am big enough, I'll tell everyone about this great race. But until then, I'll just let this light of mine shine.

This little light of mine. I'm gonna let it shine. Let it shine, let it shine, let it shine.

Sometimes when I feel afraid. You always remind of your great faith. You tell me how strong I am and that you're always there and even if I'm sad, you pat me on my back and tell me child come talk to dad.

Hebrews 13:5

Never will I leave you,
Never will I forsake you.

Even when I'm hungry and
my stomach starts to roar,
you smile right at me and say,
little one hunger no more.

                                  Matthew 6:26

Look at the birds of the air;
they do not sow or reap or
store away in barns, and yet
the father feeds them all.

You understand me in ways I've never known and you carry me like flowers in full bloom.

Jeremiah 1:5

Before I formed you in the womb I knew you.

At times when it seems like nothing is going right. You remind me of your great love and how precious I am in your great sight.

John 3:16

For God so loved the world that he gave his only begotten son, that whosoever shall believe in him shall not perish but have everlasting life.

The End

About the Author

Asia Coleman writes faith based children's books that will encourage children and people from all around the world from different backgrounds. Before she started writing books, Asia was working as an educator and a school social worker in the North Carolina School System. She has always felt that working with children was a part of her calling and she knew that God was going to do something great with the gifts that he's placed on the inside of her.

As a wife and a mother of three children and a blended family of eight. One day she was in prayer, she said the Lord began to speak to her and let her know it's time for you to write. Asia prayed that the Lord would enlarge her territory only to find out, only to find out that he would truly do so.

From that moment on, it had been epic for Asia. From the book "God and Me" to "I AM: Affirmations for Children" to "Because I know God" and "From Better to Great in the Kingdom of God", Asia has shown her ability to continue to run in this great race of faith. She believes that these books are uplifting and life changing. It's designed to bring forth hope and joy while feeling love and warmth of God's presence.

www.ingramcontent.com/pod-product-compliance
Lightning Source LLC
LaVergne TN
LVHW070047070526
838200LV00028B/416